Amazing Animal Survivors

Written by Keith Pigdon

Series Consultant: Linda Ho

WorldWise
Content-based Learning

Contents

Introduction 4

Chapter 1:
Surviving in harsh places 6
  Deserts 6
  Surviving at high altitudes 8
  Surviving the cold 10
  Adapting to harsh environments 12

Chapter 2:
Surviving in forests
and grasslands 14
  Chameleons 15
  On the grasslands 16

Chapter 3:
Hunting in the dark 18
  Seeing their prey 19
  Using heat detectors 20
  Using sound 21

Chapter 4:
Protecting themselves 22
  Hiding, poison and bad smells 22
  Looking dangerous and pretending 24
  Skin, scales, feather and fur 26
  Partnerships for protection 28

Conclusion 30

Glossary 31

Index 32

Introduction

Animals survive in most places on Earth, even in places where life is very difficult.

The difficulties vary. For some animals, it is extreme climate – hot or cold – or high altitude. Often animals live in places where there is **competition** for food and danger from **predators**. Some animals survive in dark caves.

All the animals are able to survive because they have changed to suit the conditions they face. They have adapted.

To survive, all animals need food, shelter and safety for themselves and their young. To do this, many animals have changed their bodies, the way they behave and even their **life cycles**.

Animals have been adapting to different environments ever since life on Earth began.

Chapter 1

Surviving in harsh places

Deserts

Deserts are the harshest places on Earth. They have high daytime temperatures and low nighttime temperatures, and little rainfall. Because of these conditions, there are fewer life-giving plants for animals to eat.

Camels

Camels are perfectly adapted to desert life. To protect themselves against sand, they have thick hairs in their ears, a clear thin layer over each eye and two rows of eyelashes. Their **nostrils** close when sand is blowing. Their large, wide soft feet spread their weight so they don't sink into the sand.

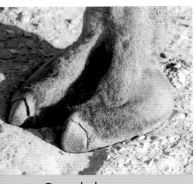

Camels have wide feet.

Find out more

Desert covers about 20 per cent of Earth. Find out where these deserts are.

6

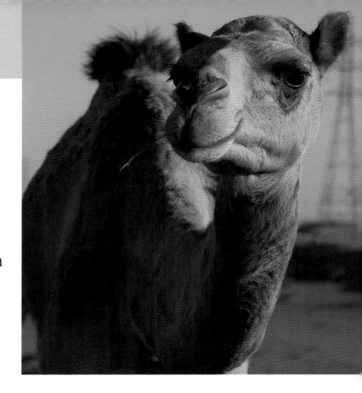

Thick fur on the top of their body protects them from the sun, and thin fur underneath allows camels to lose heat from their bodies. They are able to go for many days without water, but they can drink huge amounts of water when it is available.

Camels can save water because they rarely lose any from sweating.

The thorny devil

The Australian thorny devil has a very tough, spiky covering of scales. These scales protect it from the heat of the desert and from predators because they make this animal look dangerous to touch. The colours of the scales match the colours of the desert, making this lizard hard to see.

The spiky scales on this lizard also help it get the water it needs to survive. The lizard has tiny grooves between its scales that absorb moisture from dew and damp sand. The moisture moves along the grooves to the corners of the lizard's mouth. Thorny devils dine on small ants that are easily found in the desert.

A bar-headed goose

In summer, bar-headed geese fly over the Himalayas to breed.

Surviving at high altitudes

Bar-headed geese are the highest-flying birds in the world.

In winter, these geese live in **lowland** India, where they feed on crops such as wheat, barley and corn.

In early summer, as the breeding season approaches, the bar-headed geese fly over the Himalayan Ranges to Tibet, where it is safe for them to nest and breed and there is plenty of food. These geese are helped by the winds that blow in the same direction that they are travelling.

Bar-headed geese in India in winter

A bar-headed goose in the snow in Tibet

This flight over the Himalayas is an amazing feat. As the geese fly higher and higher, the air becomes thinner as it has less **oxygen**. It is much harder for animals to get enough oxygen from the air at high **altitudes**.

But bar-headed geese have larger lungs and can breathe faster and deeper than other geese, so they can take in more oxygen from the air. Their body muscles and their heart muscles can deal with the extra oxygen. They also have blood that can hold more oxygen.

Flying is much harder in thin air because there is less **pressure** under the wings to lift the birds upward, so they must flap their wings more.

Find out more
How high do bar-headed geese fly?

Surviving the cold

Wood frogs

Wood frogs are able to survive some of the coldest temperatures on Earth. They live in Alaska and other freezing places in the Arctic where most animals could not survive.

As the winter temperature drops below freezing, the wood frog goes into **hibernation**. It stops breathing, and its heart stops beating. It becomes mostly frozen! But it has chemicals in its blood that stop its blood from freezing and protect the heart and other main organs.

When spring returns and the temperature gets warmer, the ice around the wood frog melts and the animal begins to **thaw**. It starts to breathe, and its heart starts beating again. The wood frog becomes active and begins feeding and looking for a mate.

Musk oxen

Musk oxen live in the frozen Arctic and Greenland. Their bodies are covered in long, thick, shaggy hair, which keeps them warm. In winter, musk oxen hair hangs almost to the ground and holds in the warmth like a tent.

Musk oxen feed on wildflowers in the summer. In winter, they move up the hillsides where the snow is not too deep to feed on the roots and mosses that grow in the frozen ground. They dig for these foods with their hooves.

Two coats of hair – a long outer coat and a shorter inner coat of hollow hairs that trap body heat to help it keep warm

Large hooves with two toes to spread body weight and let it walk easily on soft snow

Small ears and short legs reduce heat loss

Musk oxen usually live in herds. When they huddle close together, they can stay warm. Living in a herd keeps them safe because they can watch for predators and can warn members of the group when there is danger.

Adapting to harsh environments

Foxes live in many environments around the world. Some, however, live in very harsh but different environments. How do they do it?

Find out more

Where do Arctic foxes live? Where do fennec foxes live?

The Arctic fox

Arctic foxes live in very cold climates, so their bodies are well suited to cold weather. Their bodies don't lose heat quickly. They have short ears, short legs and thick white fur coats to help them stay warm. Fur on their paws keeps their feet warm and stops them from slipping on ice and snow.

The fennec fox

Fennec foxes live in very hot deserts, so their bodies are well suited to hot weather. Their bodies help them lose heat quickly. They have large ears, long legs and a lighter fur coat that still keeps them warm at night. Fur on their paws protects their feet from hot sands. Fennec foxes also lose heat by panting and sweating, and they can survive in the desert with very little water.

	Arctic fox	Fennec fox
Size	Large body (2 to 3 kilograms)	Small body (up to 1.5 kilograms)
Color	Fur that is white or light grey in winter and grey brown in summer	Cream-coloured or light-brown coat that does not change with the seasons
Ears	Short, round ears to stop heat loss	Very large ears to cool body and help them hear **prey** burrowing in sand
Coat	Very thick coat of fur	Lighter coat
Paws	Fur on paws to protect feet from cold	Fur on paws to stop burning

Chapter 2

Surviving in forests and grasslands

Animals can survive much more easily in forests and grasslands than in places that are very hot or cold. This is because forests and grasslands have habitats and climates that are animal friendly and provide lots of food choices. There are many ways for animals to protect themselves and raise their young.

But living in forests and grasslands means that there are many more species and much larger numbers of animals competing for survival in the same spaces.

The smallest chameleon is about five centimetres long, and the largest grows to 60 centimetres.

A chameleon can move its eyes in different directions.

Find out more

A chameleon's tongue is one and a half times longer than its body. Which other animals have very long tongues?

Chameleons

Chameleons are slow-moving reptiles that mainly live in trees in forests. So how does a slow-moving lizard that lives in trees catch enough food to survive and not get eaten?

Chameleons can easily change colour. This makes it harder for their **predators** and their **prey** to see them. They remain very still and can change the colour of their scales to match the colours around them. This is called **camouflage**.

Chameleons also have incredible eyes. Without moving their heads, they can move their eyes to see in every direction. Also, each eye can move separately from the other. So the left eye can look forward, while the right eye looks backward.

Without moving, the chameleon can watch its prey come closer. When the insect gets close enough – zap! The chameleon extends and wraps its huge tongue around its prey.

Find out more

Most predators hunt alone. Which predators hunt in groups, and why do they do that?

On the grasslands

Many animals live together on grasslands where there is plenty of food. Many of these animals are plant eaters. They are prey for animal hunters – predators. Both types of animals have adapted to survive.

Predators

To survive in grasslands, predators are well adapted to catch prey. Predators such as the cheetah have bodies that are built to move at a frightening speed. Lions and leopards can also move fast over very short distances. They must get close to the animals they are hunting before they make a chase.

These animals have eyes in the front of their heads so that they can judge the size and distance of their prey. Their body colours camouflage them in long grass so they can stalk their prey until they get close enough to attack. They have sharp teeth and claws to kill and eat their prey.

Lion hunting

Cheetah running

Prey

Many animals that are hunted by predators have adaptations to help them avoid being caught. They often live in groups. They have eyes on the sides of their heads so they can see all around them. Their fur acts as a camouflage in the long grass.

Prey animals such as pronghorn antelopes can move fast. They have strong bodies and fast-moving muscles that help them avoid being caught.

Herd of impala

Large herds of grassland animals such as pronghorn antelopes and impala travel long distances each year in search of food as the seasons change. This is important if they are to survive.

Pronghorn antelope

Find out more

Prey animals breed when the number of predators is low and there is plenty of food.

Predators breed when there are plenty of prey animals nearby to feed their young.

How do these animals care for their young?

This snake hunts at night.

Chapter 3

Hunting in the dark

Animals that rest during the daytime and feed at night are called nocturnal animals. Nocturnal animals are well adapted to survive in dark places.

Their body colours and shapes protect them from predators as they are very hard to see at night. But they need to be able to find and catch their food in the dark, and they have many ways of doing that.

The greater galago hunts at night. Its wide-open eyes enable it to see in the dark.

Owls have larger eyes than most other birds.

Seeing their prey

Some nocturnal animals have very large eyes that allow them to see in very dim light. Owls and geckos are large-eyed animals that hunt in the dark.

Geckos have much larger eyes than lizards that hunt during the day.

Using heat detectors

Some animals can find their **prey** in the dark without using their eyes. Snakes can find their prey in the dark. Snakes sense the small changes in temperature that warm-blooded prey cause as they move around in the dark.

Pythons and vipers have heat-seeking pit organs in their jaws. These pit organs sense heat just like burglar alarms and security lights do.

pit organ

Using sound

Bats use their sharp hearing to help find their way around and to find their food. Bats send out high-pitched sounds. The time the echo takes to return to their ears tells the bats where objects and their prey are in their habitat. Bats have large ears and special **vocal cords** to help them do this.

A leaf-tailed gecko

Chapter 4

Protecting themselves

Most animals need to have ways of protecting themselves from predators. Some have developed bodies that are hard to see or have behaviours that make it difficult for their **predators** or **prey** to notice them. Others have bodies that can harm predators.

Running away from danger is often the best defence for speedy animals. But some animals can't move quickly or are too young to run fast. Some of these animals protect themselves by keeping perfectly still and quiet so that a predator may not see or hear them.

Hiding, poison and bad smells

A number of animals including insects, fish, frogs and toads have chemicals in their bodies that are poisonous to other animals that eat them. Predators die when they eat the poison dart frog. The monarch butterfly is poisonous to birds and lizards that try to eat it.

A poison dart frog

A poisonous cobra

Other animals make poison in their bodies that is injected when their spines are touched or they use their fangs. The stonefish and the butterfly cod have sharp spines that inject poison into anything that contacts them. Some snakes, spiders and insects use their venom to defend themselves or to catch their prey.

A few animals copy the markings of poisonous or venomous animals to fool predators. The danaid eggfly butterfly protects itself by copying the markings of the monarch so that it will be mistaken for a poisonous butterfly. This is called mimicry.

A small number of animals deal with threats by making the attacker look for something else to eat. When threatened, some millipedes can attack by spraying a very smelly substance that is rich in acid. Turkey vultures are known to vomit any smelly undigested meat in their stomach when they feel threatened. The vomit smells terrible and can sting the skin and eyes of the predator.

A turkey vulture

A danaid eggfly butterfly copies the markings of the poisonous monarch butterfly.

23

Looking dangerous and pretending

You might have noticed that cats fluff themselves up and stand as tall as they can when they fear a dog. They try to make themselves appear bigger to scare the dog away. When threatened, the frilled lizard opens its large mouth, makes a hissing whistle and extends the skins around its neck. This makes it look very fierce and a lot larger.

Some animals have long sharp spines to prevent attackers from harming them. Hedgehogs and echidnas are covered with spikes. When threatened, echidnas quickly dig a hole with their sharp claws so that only their spines can be seen.

A frilled lizard in a threatening pose.

An echidna has long sharp spines

A ladybird

Many animals that can sting or bite have red or yellow body colours. These bright colours warn a predator that an animal can sting or be poisonous. Many insects defend themselves by using bright colours. Many wasps and bees have black and yellow stripes. Ladybirds are orange with black spots to warn predators that they are not good to eat.

When a predator approaches, lapwings and plovers pretend to be wounded. They run away from their nest dragging a wing and pretending that they can't fly. This draws the predator away from the young or eggs towards the parent that is faking injury.

A lapwing

The Arctic hare in summer (left) and winter (right)

Skin, scales, feathers and fur

All animals need body coverings that protect them and help them to survive in their habitats and environment. Their bodies are covered with either skin, fur (hair), feathers, or scales.

All mammals have fur or hair. In colder climates, mammals usually have two coats of fur. In winter, a thick coat serves as insulation, keeping body heat in and cold out. This heavy coat falls out in warm weather and is replaced by a thinner summer coat. This is called moulting.

Birds are different to other animals because of their feathers. Feathers are needed for them to fly, keep warm, keep dry, hide and find a mate. Birds like penguins that live in cold places have more feathers than most other birds. They have about ten feathers per square centimetre. The feathers are curved and lap over each other like roof tiles. This helps the water run off them quickly.

A close-up of the feathers of King penguins

A close-up of scales of a snake

Reptiles have skin that is covered with dry scales. These scales protect their bodies and stop them from losing too much water and drying out. Some reptiles have very thick scales. Fish are also covered with scales that protect their skin and keep the water out of their bodies.

Frogs and toads have bare skin without any feathers, fur or scales. These animals breathe through their skin which must be kept moist.

A green tree frog

27

A pair of black-backed jackals

Partnerships for protection

Some animals are able to survive by being alone for most of their lives. Other animals are always seen in pairs or larger numbers. Living in groups helps them protect themselves. Sometimes living with just a partner that can see, smell and hear gives extra protection.

Animals like black-backed jackals live in pairs and stay together for life. They travel, hunt and raise their young together.

A herd of buffalos

Buffalo on the African plains are always found in large herds. When faced with a stalking pride of lions they stand close together in a circle with their heads down and their powerful horns pointing towards their attackers.

Many kinds of small fish travel in huge schools as a way of protecting themselves against predators.

A school of fish

An ox pecker on the back of a buffalo

Some animals have a kind of partnership with other animal species.

Ox peckers feed on ticks filled with blood that they find on the skins of zebras, giraffes, hippopotamuses and buffaloes. The animals they live on are called hosts. Ox peckers help their hosts by removing these harmful parasites from their bodies.

Ants on aphids

Aphids suck sap from the leaves and shoots of plants. From this sap they make a sweet liquid called honey dew. Ants are able to make the aphids release their honey dew, by stroking the aphids' bodies. The honey dew is then used as food in the ants nest.

The stinging tentacles of the sea anemone are home to the clown fish. They are not harmed by these tentacles but predators dare not enter this dangerous place. The sea anemone feeds on scraps of food left by the fish.

Clown fish among sea anemones

Conclusion

All the animal species that are alive today have survived because they have been able to adapt to their habitats and their environments. Over time, their bodies have changed in ways that help them to get the food and shelter they need, to protect themselves from **predators**, and to be successful in raising their young. Many have also changed the way they behave to allow them to live successfully.

Animal species that cannot adapt to their changing environment do not survive. They die out and become extinct.

Glossary

altitudes regions or areas found high above ground level

camouflage the ability of animals to blend into their surroundings by using colouring, markings or skin texture. When an animal uses camouflage, other animals have difficulty seeing it.

competition when two or more living things have the same need, such as food, and that need is scarce or difficult to get

hibernation to become inactive throughout winter, by slowing down body systems

life cycles the stages that a living thing goes though, from the beginning of its life to the beginning of its offspring's life

lowland an area that is lower than surrounding land. Lowlands are often flat or at sea level.

nostrils the openings in the nose through which living things breathe

oxygen a gas found in the air around us, which people and animals need to survive

predators animals that get food by killing and eating other animals

pressure a force pushing on something

prey an animal that is caught and eaten by another animal

thaw to slowly move out of a frozen state

vocal cords a pair of stretchy bands inside the throat that help produce sound

Index

ants 29

aphids 29

Arctic fox 12, 13

bar-headed geese 8–9

bat 21

black-backed jackals 28

buffalo 28, 29

camel 6–7

camouflage 15, 16, 17, 23

chameleon 15

cheetah 16

claws 16

clown fish 29

danaid eggfly butterfly 23

desert 6, 7, 12

ears 6, 11, 12, 13, 21

echidnas 24

eyes 6, 15, 16, 17, 18, 19, 20

feathers 27

fennec fox 12, 13

food 4, 5, 8, 11, 14, 15, 16, 17, 18, 21, 22, 23

forests 14, 15

frilled lizard 24

fur 7, 12, 13, 17, 26, 27

gecko 19

grasslands 14, 16, 17

hair 6, 11

hedgehogs 24

herd 11, 17

hibernation 10, 23

hooves 11

impala 17

ladybirds 25

lapwings 25

leopard 16

lion 16

lizard 7, 15, 19

millipedes 23

mimicry 23

monarch butterfly 22, 23

moulting 26

musk oxen 11

owl 19

ox peckers 29

paws 12, 13

plovers 25

poison dart frog 22

pronghorn antelope 17

scales 7, 15, 27

sea anemone 29

shelter 5, 22

snake 18, 20

teeth 16

tentacles 29

thorny devil 7

wood frog 10